The Little Book of Prosperity:

A guide to creating everyday

abundance financially and

spiritually

By Christina Hughes

© *2009 Christina Hughes*

This work may not be reproduced in any

form without the author's permission

4

From the fullness of his grace we have all received one

blessing after another. John 1:16 NIV

I will celebrate your abundant goodness and joyfully

sing of your righteousness. Psalm 145:7

Thank you to the Lord, spirit and my angels in

heaven and here on earth. Thank you to my mom for

5

always believing in me. Thank you to Damian my

soul mate for always inspiring me and encouraging

me. Thank you to Mariel Hemingway for bringing me

back to my yoga/meditation practice. Thank you to

my church for always inspiring me to be the best that

I can be. Thank you to Silver Ravenwolf and Fiona

Horn for your wonderful books may spirit always

bless you.

Introduction: I am so pleased you picked up my book

and have decided to join me on this journey. I am not

rich and I don't proclaim to be. But, I do know there is a lot more to prosperity and abundance then money. I always have enough when I need it. I try not to focus on the lack in my life. I try to be grateful for many things. I realize I am blessed in many ways. When I first started my journey I didn't really Believe that was the case. I've struggled financially and I've struggled with depression. I got through it with my faith and spirituality. That is the real goal and aim for this book. I hope this book becomes a daily inspiration for you in your life. All these tools have helped me to gain abundance in my life financially but even more importantly spiritually as well. If you are ready to take this journey let's get started.

Chapter 1- yoga and meditation

You might be asking yourselves how yoga and

meditation will help me gain prosperity. While the

truth is it won't outright help you gain prosperity. But

it will help you to focus on the present so you don't get

so tangled up in your financial situation that you

keep thinking negatively because that won't help your

financial situation at all. Sometimes it's good to just

take a step back relax and see if we can find a new

perspective on the situation. I find that yoga and

meditation really help when it comes to that.

There are many different styles of yoga so I won't go

into them all here. I will say if yoga is something you might be interested in trying there are many classes and books on the subject. I will be recommending some at the end of this chapter.

There are also many forms of meditation. I will be going into some of the basics. First you can sit with legs crossed in Lotus position or sitting in a comfortable chair you can also lie down if you like but try not to fall asleep. Then you can just sit and watch your breath. Listen as you breathe in and out. Try to take long deep breaths versus the shorter breaths we normally take. You can also count numbers in your head you can count up to ten and start all over again or count as high as you possibly can. You can also gaze at a candle if keeping your eyes closed is too hard for you or is not something you

feel comfortable with yet. These are just some basic

meditations to get you started I recommend you read

a more informative book or even take a meditation

class. Also yoga classes usually do meditations as well

after the workout, which is when I recommend you

meditate but any time is fine. I find it especially

helpful when I'm stressed out and need to focus on

something besides my troubles and anxiety. So I'll just

close my eyes and quickly focus on my breathe it

works really well and I can go about my day until I

have more time to do my yoga and meditation

practice.

I know it can be hard to find time to do yoga and

meditation but even taking 10 minutes a day is worth

it. I find I have a lot of energy going through my head

at the end of the day and I love to just meditate, take

deep breaths, and do yoga poses. Hatha yoga is the

simplest there is also power yoga and Ashantanga

yoga. Contrary to what some think yoga is a very

demanding exercise regimen. I find for people just

starting a yoga practice Hatha is the best yoga

practice. Then as you get more experienced you can

move on to harder yoga practices like power yoga,

Ashtanga yoga, or Brikam yoga (A type of yoga where

you do yoga in a heated room. I've never tried it but I

hear you sweat like crazy and it's a hard but very

rewarding form of yoga.)

11

Recommended reading: Mariel Hemingway's finding

my balance and Healthy living from the inside out

Very good books to learn the basic yoga and

meditation techniques there are also many other

books out there as well on both subjects and classes at

your local recreation center.

Chapter 2- Feng Shui

I have seen feng shui work for me and I've seen it work for other people otherwise I would not be writing this book right now. I worry about money just like everyone else just about does. I think it's normal to worry about prosperity but you also don't want to focus on lack. Feng shui is fairly simple you don't have to know much about it. I suggest you start by implementing small changes at first and then go from there.

If you walk into the room from the west then your prosperity section would be in the left corner of the room.

First and foremost you want your house to be clean

and organized. Energy gets cluttered and stagnant

and needs to flow. If you have a messy house it's

easier for the energy to get stagnant. If you do need to

organize and clean don't go crazy with it just start

with one corner at a time and do what you can. You

will be amazed at how just cleaning can change the

flow of energy and you can start having

improvements in your life.

Some simple things for prosperity:

Sound is a great way to create prosperity in your life.

Wind chimes are very good and bells.

Light is another way. You can light a green candle

(This also goes with candle magick in spells.) You can

also put a lamp in the area. By doing this it helps to

liven the chi of the area.

Mirrors can be used as a cure for almost any area of the house. Just be careful as you don't want mirrors reflecting clutter. Make sure the mirror is at face level and not above or below your head.

Plants flowers and living things increase chi. you can put a green plant or flower in this area. Just replace new plants or flowers when the old one dies and try to constantly water it.

Heavy objects are good when you feel like your prosperity is slipping away but be careful if the energy starts to feel stuck or stagnant then change the area up.

If things are already good for you in the prosperity area then you don't have to go crazy even if things are not so good for you then please just remember to take it slow. One item and one step at a time, I know you are probably eager to gain prosperity but doing one thing at a time will help tremendously.

I know feng shui has helped me and I believe that it can help you as well.

Some Recommended reading:

Clear you're Clutter with feng shui by Karen Kingston

Creating sacred space with feng shui by Karen Kingston

Move your stuff change your life by Karen Rauch Carter

Chapter 3- Vastu

Vastu originated in India. Vastu is actually even older then feng shui. In India people use vastu to build their homes and buildings. They do that for two reasons. The first is because they believe it does make their lives better and more functional. Second because it also makes the buildings more stable. Many temples built this way are still standing today.

Vastu is for any religion. You don't have to practice Hinduism or ayer veda an Indian health system to practice vastu. You do have to set up alters and say mantras and do mudras. But, you don't have to place a picture of a specific deity on your alter or pray to

one if you don't feel comfortable doing so.

In vastu your prosperity alters goes in the north

section of the room preferably against a west-facing

wall. You can use a self, window sill, or table to put

up your alter. I suggest using a green or gold cloth

those are prosperity colors. Try to incorporate green

and gold items on your alter.

How to place items on you're alter:

The air symbol goes in the northwest part of your

alter. My air symbol is an incense holder. You can

also use a fan, a feather, and a statue of a bird or

angel. Be creative with your symbols and use what

means the most to you.

The water symbol goes in the northeast sector on your

alter. I've used a clear cup with a glass of spring

water. You can use a green or gold vase and a green

plant just make sure you can see the water through

the vase.

The earth element goes in the southwest sector on

your alter. I've used a plant. You can also use a statue

of the goddess Lakshmi or Hindu god Ganesha. You

can also use stones or anything from earth.

The fire element goes in the southeast section of your

alter. I've used a green candle. You can use a green or

gold candle in this area.

Your personal symbol goes in the back of your alter.

I've used a gold paper brick to symbolize prosperity

and a picture of the Hindu goddess Lakshmi. You can

use whatever represents prosperity to you after all it is

your personal symbol.

For the offering tray I've used a green plate with the words written on a piece of paper abundance, prosperity, and wealth. You should use a green or gold plate or bowl. A small tray with whatever kind of words on a piece of paper that you want to bring into your life or you can just write prosperity and abundance on the pieces of paper.

How to activate you're alter:

Before you do the ritual make sure you take a shower and wear clean clothes. Or at least wash your face and hands.

You may sit or stand at your alter. Light the candle and incense if you have any. Ring bells if you have any on your alter. Take ten to twelve deep breaths.

Experience the feeling of abundance and prosperity in your life like you already have it but don't think about anything specific.

Use your right hand hold your pinky and index finger together holding your other fingers down with your thumb. Move your hand backward and forward nine times. Chanting om budhaye namaha om boo da hay na ma haa.

How to keep you're alter ignited:

Take some time to pray and meditate at your alter. Make sure you change the flowers and take care of any plants if you choose to use them.

How to create your own alter for any purpose:

You can create an alter for any purpose. There are many reasons people create altars. I've created an alter to reminded me of my own beauty and to be

confident in my femininity and myself. I've created

an alter with pictures of family and friends.

The first thing before creating an alter is to set your

intention. It can be anything you want. It's

completely up to you.

Some examples are:

Pay homage to a desist pet, friend, or relative (I have

an alter dedicated to my past on loved ones and

animals)

To find inspiration

Make a petition

Gather healing energies

Communicate with a deity

22

Create or honor change in your life like:

Birth

Death

Marriage

Divorce

Moving into a new home

To bring good luck

Be creative

Write your dreams

Appreciate beauty in yourself, nature, and life

Bring abundance and prosperity

Honor the seasons

Be still and meditate

Perform magick

Anything that means something to you

Where to place your altars:

One of my alters is on a window sill and another is on

a table in my bedroom and another is on a built in

shelf.

You can place your altars anywhere. It can be placed

in a private area of your home or out for everyone to

see. Some examples of where you can place you're

alter are:

On a dresser

In your kitchen

Windowsill

On a hope chest

On a fireplace

Around a mirror

Garden outdoors or green room

Tabletop

Desktop

Inside a cupboard

Any place indoors that feels important to you

Things you can place on your altars:

On my alter I have candles, perfume bottles, a bowl

with petals floating in water. My other alter I have

pictures of my decided love ones and a candle. I have

another alter with candles, statue, water and a table

cloth.

Examples of what you can place on you're alters:

Candles

Incense

Seashells

Flowers

Gifts and cards

Written petitions

Masks

Musical instruments

Wine glass

Bowls of water

Statues

Photos and pictures

Lights

Scarves and cloths

Gems, stones, and crystals

Plants

A journal:

A dream journal

A psychic notebook

Book of shadows

Notebook with poems or songs

Tarot cards and rune stones

Anything important to you

When to change you're alter: if you have flowers of

live elements like plants you should change those.

Otherwise you can change it around whenever you

feel it needs a change. It can be a candle, a tablecloth,

pictures, or anything else that means something to

you.

You can change you're alter:

Seasonally

At the full moon or new moon

Weekly

When you stop noticing it as much

Never

You take things down and put them up at whim

What to do at you're alter:

At one of my alters I pray and another one I talk to

my deceased loved ones and remember them.

You can:

Sing

Chant

Meditate

Recite mantras and affirmations

Read

Write poems and songs

Connect with divinity

Dance

Decorate with jewelry

Yoga

Sit quietly

Divination:

Tarot cards and runes

Pray

Play an instrument

Ring a bell or hit a gong

Listen to music

Spray perfume

Burn incense

Arrange flowers

Put perfume or oil on

Write

Write affirmations

I hope you have enjoyed this chapter on alters and

Vastu.

Recommended reading:

Alters of power and Grace by Robin and Michael

Mastro

A book of women's alters by Nancy Brady

Cunningham and Denise Gedden

Part 4

Spells and magick

Spells and magick are supposed to be fun but before

we begin I must warn you they are also serious

business. If you don't feel comfortable doings spells

you don't have to. But, you can do spells no matter

what your religion. We've all heard about the laws of

attraction and praying. Spells are almost the same

thing. But, they should be taken seriously. So there

are a few basic things to know before casting magick

and doing spells.

1. Be careful what you wish because it might actually come true. Always make sure you know what you want the outcome of the spell to be before you do the spell.

2. One of the biggest and post important is to harm none. Whatever you put into your spells you will get back weather for better or worse. And don't manipulate others emotions. Always end with May this spell not reverse or place upon me any curse, with harm to none, so mote it be!

3. When you do the spell think more of the

feelings of having prosperity or your

intention but don't think about how you will

get it or the specific outcome of a situation.

That is up to spirit how it will manifest not

you. Also that goes into a form of

manipulation so it's better to be weary of

thinking specifics and focus on the feeling.

How to set up you're alter:

Most items on the alter for doing spell work or up the

person. You will usually have an alter cloth

correlating to the season or the type of spell in this

case prosperity would be a green or gold cloth. You

also want to have the elements on your table. The

elements should be set up like this: in the north

section is earth (this can be dirt from outside or salt

from your kitchen cupboard) on the east of the table

is air (you can use incense, a feather, or a bell.) On

the south side of your alter is fire (this can be a

candle. Make sure you don't leave it unattended.)

The west is for water (you can have a bowl or cup of

water I suggest bottled or spring. You want the water

to be as pure as possible.) Then you can also place a

black and white candle on your alter. But, this is not

a necessity. And a statue or picture of your chosen

deity or none if you like you can also do projects on

your alter and leave them there until complete for a

blessing. Or save the items you use for spell work until

you manifest your goals and then burn or bury the

items to ground them. Just make sure not to clutter

your alter and to clean it up after doing spell work.

Once you've set up your alter it's time to cleanse and consecrate your items. You can take your items and run them through sage incense or buy a sage smudge sticks to cleanse and purify the alter say you want to cleanse the salt say "I cleanse this salt of all negativity may this salt be used for positive purposes and bring positive results and all negativity flee away." Then sprinkle it around your alter and do the same with the other items in a clockwise direction. Then your stuff is cleansed and consecrated that's all there is too it.

Before you do the spells make sure you do grounding and centering? You want to be calm and relaxed and so you might want to meditate and do some yoga. Or listen to some calming soothing music. You don't

want to work magick when you are under stress of

upset. You want to try to be as calm as possible.

Then you don't have to necessarily work magick in a

sacred circle. Sometimes with time constraints that is

just not feasible. But, when you can't it's still good to

at least ground yourself and picture a big protective

bubble around you and your space it's like your

armor to keep all the negativity out. This does not

mean things that go bump in the night but sometimes

from other people or even ourselves there are negative

debris around. If you have time to cast a circle you

can use your finger, a wand, or athame (a special

knife used for magical purposes and no it does not

involve anything evil like animals sacrifices.

Personally I would never condone that and that has no part in magick and spells.) Walk in a clockwise circle three times chanting something like: I conjure the circle to protect my space and me. May the angels (or whomever you choose) protect this sacred circle and keep all negativity out of this magick realm. Nothing can enter that I do not want to. So mote it be! And then stomp your foot on the ground and say "this circle is sealed." Now you have your magick circle. When you take it down walk counterclockwise once picturing the energy going into your finger, wand, or athame and you can put it in your magick items your alter your familiar or anything that is significant.

Basic candle magick spells for prosperity: You need a

green candle. Carve in the word prosperity and your

name into the candle. Light the candle and feel

yourself having prosperity. What would you do with

the money? What do you need it for? Don't think of

how you will get it just the feeling of having it.

Meditate on this for as long as possible. Then say

"with harm to none, so mote it be!" When you are

done put the candle out with a candlesnuffer don't

blow the candle out. Then light the candle everyday

until you get your prosperity. Then bury the wax to

ground the energy. Or if you like you can also let the

candle burn out and then bury the wax. Repeat as

needed.

Petition magick for prosperity:

You write down on a piece of paper what you want

provided it won't harm anyone or control anyone's

emotions and then burn the paper, Say with harm to

none, so mote it be!

Spells for prosperity and success should preferable be

done on Thursdays. On Thursday it's a good day to

wear green clothing.

I hope you found this chapter insightful. Here is some

recommended reading if you want

to know more:

Teen witch by Silver Ravenwolf

To ride a silver broomstick by Silver Ravenwolf

Earth, air, fire and water by Scott Cunningham

7 days to a magickal new you by Fiona Horn

Witch by Fiona Horn

Book of shadows by Phyllis Currott

The craft by Dorothy Morrison

Workplace spells by Marla Brooks

Part 5 Prayer

No matter what your religious beliefs are you can always pray. You don't need to be spiritual to say affirmations but they are incredibly effective for changing your mindset.

I believe greatly in prayer and affirmation you don't want to beg but you do want to be grateful for what you have. Then you can ask for the things you want. An example:

Thank you _ for my family, friends, for the money and prosperity that I do have. I know you have given me everything that I have and I'm grateful. I am not in want. Please provide me with the financial stability

that I need to provide for my family and myself.

Thank you for blessing me with the gift of prosperity

in my life.

You can also use affirmations like:

I have everything that I need in my life. I have

prosperity and abundance. I am able to provide for

my family and myself.

For more on prayer there are many good books out

there. Some recommendations are:

You can heal your life by Louise Hay

.

Science and health with keys to the scriptures by

Mary Baker Eddy

A course in Miracles

Awakening to your true purpose By Eckhart Tolle

Starting your day right Devotions for each day of the

morning by Joyce Meyer

The secret to true Happiness by Joyce Meyer

100 ways to simplify your life by Joyce Meyer

Never give up by Joyce Meyer

The power of a praying woman by Stormie

 Omartian

Part 6- The Law of Attraction

This concept has been around for centuries.

Unfortunately for a long time not many people really

understood how it worked. As times goes on great

minds, writer, philosophers, and scientists are

discovering that the thoughts we think control our

emotions and our emotions control our outer

environment. Don't you ever feel a sense of negativity

after being around a complaining negative person

and once you get out of that environment you are

much happier and things seem to be better

emotionally. That's because the other person is

dragging you down. When you are around positive

people and in a positive environment you feel more

positive. It's the same thing with our thoughts. Not

that we can control every thought that comes through

our minds we have thousands a day, But, there are

some techniques that can help.

Some of the ones I've already mentioned prayer,

affirmations, yoga, meditation are great ways to get

control of our thoughts and mind sets. Sometimes you

just have to take yourself out of a negative situation.

Also the circle technique and can help when you are

around negative people and feeling stressed out.

Think prosperity and feel prosperity and it will come.

I had a situation where I had to pay some bills and I was stressing out about it. But, then I prayed and did my affirmations that helped to change my mind set. Then I focused on prosperity and had the feeling of having the money paying the bills and all being well. I focused on that all day as many times as I could and at the end of the day I had the money I needed to pay the bills.

Recommended reading:

The secret by Rhonda Byrne

The circle by Laura Day

The Passion test by Janet Bray and Chris Attwood

Afterward:

I hope you enjoyed reading this book. I have given

you many examples of bringing more prosperity in

your life. I wish you joy, happiness, prosperity, and a

bit of good magick in your life. It has been an exciting

journey writing this book. I put a lot of effort into it. If

I can help even one person then it will be worth it to

have written this book.

I am currently working on my next book: Shine: A

memoir

49

Acknowledgements:

It took me a long time to write this book. I am still

working on this book. I wan to help people and

share what I've learned. I am still learning and will

always be learning how to grow spiritually. I think

that is the beauty of life. I want to thank my higher

power for letting me share my work with others in

whatever way I can. To my mom for supporting me.

My grandma Jeanne for supporting me in this

endeavor. Damian for accepting me as I am and

always being proud of me. And especially to you

dear reader I hope your pathway is always blessed

with prosperity and everyday abundance.

1323955R0

Printed in Great Britain by
Amazon.co.uk, Ltd.,
Marston Gate.